There Shall be a PERFORMANCE

Biodun Olaitan

There shall be a Performance
Copyright © **2011 Biodun Olaitan**
First Printed in 2009
All rights reserved

No part of this publication may be reproduced or transmitted in any form or by any means, electronic or mechanical, including photocopying, recording, or any information storage and retrieval systems, without permission in writing from the author and publisher.

''Extracts from the Authorised Version of the Bible (The King James Bible), the rights in which are vested in the Crown, are reproduced by permission of the Crown's Patentee, Cambridge University Press.''

Email: **nifepelumi@yahoo.co.uk**
Phone: **07500048655**

Printed in Great Britain

SOS Publications
www.SOSPublications.com
SOSPublications@yahoo.com

Dedication

To God, my creator who gave me the grace and revelation about this book.

Foreword

The story of Joseph is a classic episode that cuts across every aspect of life and ministry. From his gifting to interpret dreams, to his incarceration and his ultimate promotion; he went through the crucible of rejection, loneliness and false accusation. These unavoidable afflictions eventually produced in him patience and total dependence upon God.

This book gives an insight into the various aspects of Joseph's life: starting with his gifting to his exaltation. This piece of writing would reveal the fact that no man is anything by himself.

Every aspect of man's greatness lies in his ability to surrender his will to God and allow the Holy Spirit to work through him. As you read and reflect on the various aspects of this book, put yourself in the picture and discover aspects that may describe your situation.

I pray that you will receive illumination as you read prayerfully - may your gift take you to a higher ground in Jesus name - Amen.

Pastor Ayo Adeloye,
RCCG, Nigeria.

Acknowledgements

I will like to thank God – my father for calling me into His vineyard to serve. May His name be exalted. I will also want to thank my dear and loving wife, Adejoke, who has been a great inspiration to my life and ministry – as well as a great friend, loving mother, counsellor and coworker; I love you. I will also like to express my appreciation to my wonderful gifts from God: Olorunifemi and Oluwapelumi; for their unflinching support and prayers. May God bless these rare gems.

I will like to thank my father in the Lord, General Overseer, Peace Intercessors Ministries, Prophet Sam Abraham; my mentor, counsellor and coach.

I will also like to thank my Daddy, General Overseer of The Redeemed Christian

Church of God, Pastor E. A. Adeboye, for giving me the opportunity to learn and serve under him. I also appreciate the support of my special friend Pastor Bisi Adewale who encouraged me into writing this piece. My sincere thanks to Pastor Eric Obele,

Pastor Sina Adeoti, Pastor Ranti Oyewale – may God bless you all for your prayers and encouragement.

Contents

Dedication
Forward
Acknowledgements
Prologue   10

Chapter One
The gift in a man   16
Chapter Two
Purity: The Key to Greatness   26
Chapter Three
God's Equality to Men   36
Chapter Four
The Reality of the future (Imagination)   46
Chapter Five
Opposition against our Vision   60
Chapter Six
There shall be a Performance   64
Chapter Seven
Forgiveness   72
Chapter Eight
Love Your Enemies   82
Chapter Nine
Exploring the five Pillars linked with Joseph   90

Quote

And blessed *is* she that believed: for there shall be a performance of those things which were told her from the Lord. Luke1:45

Prologue

From Dreams to Reality:
An Exposition on Joseph, the dreamer

From the Genesis account: Cast your mind to important events in the life of Joseph - remember that his brothers stripped him of his coat of many colours and cast him into a pit. We are told that the pit was empty; there was no water in it. Joseph was not killed but was rather sold for twenty pieces of Silver to a company of Ishmeelites heading to Egypt. The Midianites in turn sold him to Potiphar; Pharaoh's officer and captain of the guard.

Note that the LORD was with Joseph and his master saw that the LORD *was* with him and made all that he did to prosper in his hand. Joseph found grace in his sight and he served him: and he made him overseer and

God blessed the Egyptian's house for Joseph's sake - positively affecting all his goods and increasing his wealth.

Imagine that he left all that he had in Joseph's hands – what a great responsibility. So it came to pass, that his master's wife cast her eyes upon Joseph and asked Joseph to lie with her. But he refused - considering the fact that he would not like to do such a wicked thing to his master who had committed so much to his hands. Moreover, he did not want to sin against God. She tried to force Joseph into the very act of immorality but he fled.

Notice that this was not a one off pressure – it was consistent; and she failed woefully to achieve her aim. So she put a final pressure and the young man fled – thinking that he was free from her – but she had a plan - accusing Joseph of a crime he never committed in the first place. Joseph was sent to jail – period – but he was in a special prison – a place where the king's prisoners *were* bound.

In all these, God was with Joseph, and showed him mercy, giving him favour in the sight of the keeper of the prison. Once again, he was given an immense responsibility as the keeper of the prison committed all the prisoners in the prison to Joseph's hands. The Bible clearly says that your gift will make room for you – what a performance.

God opened the door of his prison to interpret Pharaoh's dreams. God had a plan - God planted the dreams in Pharaoh, God had an interpreter in Joseph - God had a carefully orchestrated plan - it was followed by a grand performance. Pray that God would turn all the positive and negative happenings in your life into a grand performance that will give glory to God.

Note that God also planted and plotted all the characters and activities that led Joseph to stand in the presence of another high authority once again; this time, a royalty - a King. From the level of interpreting dreams, God promoted Joseph to the position of a counsellor who gave very wise counsel to the king on how to avoid the impending famine that Pharaoh dreamt about.

Who was the discreet and wise man that Joseph counselled the King to get? Joseph. So Joseph indirectly devised his own Person's Spec for the job he was given to do. Do not be fooled – God was in the centre of it all - just like God is the author and finisher of our faith. God put the words in his mouth. Note that except the Lord intervenes in anything, we will only labour in vain; sometimes we stumble in the dark, thinking that we know it all; but God is the master planner?

> Genesis 41:
> *33 Now therefore let Pharaoh look out a man discreet and wise, and set him over the land of Egypt. 34 Let Pharaoh do this, and let him appoint officers over the land, and take up the*

fifth part of the land of Egypt in the seven plenteous years.

35 And let them gather all the food of those good years that come, and lay up corn under the hand of Pharaoh, and let them keep food in the cities. 36 And that food shall be for store to the land against the seven years of famine, which shall be in the land of Egypt; that the land perish not through the famine. 37 And the thing was good in the eyes of Pharaoh, and in the eyes of all his servants. 38 And Pharaoh said unto his servants, Can we find such a one as this is, a man in whom the Spirit of God is? 39 And Pharaoh said unto Joseph, Forasmuch as God hath showed thee all this, there is none so discreet and wise as thou art: 40 Thou shalt be over my house, and according unto thy word shall all my people be ruled: only in the throne will I be greater than thou.

41 And Pharaoh said unto Joseph, See, I have set thee over all the land of Egypt. 42 And Pharaoh took off his ring from his hand, and put it upon Joseph's hand, and arrayed him in vestures of fine linen, and put a gold chain about his neck; 43 And he made him to ride in the second chariot which he had; and they cried before him, Bow the knee: and he made him ruler over all the land of Egypt.

44 And Pharaoh said unto Joseph, I am Pharaoh, and without thee shall no man lift up his hand or foot in all the land of Egypt.

In all these, Joseph was only thirty years old when he stood before Pharaoh, King of Egypt.

Chapter One

THE GIFT IN A MAN...

"And Joseph dreamed a dream and he told it his brethren, they hated him yet the more." Genesis 37:5:

I strongly believe that everybody is gifted by God; and this comes with varied talents that can be put in use in many excellent ways. There is no man on the face of this Earth without a gift or talent. However, there is the need to develop and desire to push. Most folks who are not assertive or pushful are often held back. Why? This is because they have not put the gifts that they have been given into use.

So on a daily basis, there are many gifted people sitting on their gifts and talents - they are hardly getting anywhere; they remain stagnant and in most cases do not have a clue of what to do. If you look carefully, you will associate them with great dreams and talents. What have they done with their great dreams? God is the one that gives dreams and visions liberally - freely. They are quality gifts from God, our creator and giver of all good things.

From the Dictionary perspective, dreams may be defined as a series of images, ideas, emotions, and sensations occurring involuntarily in the mind during certain stages of sleep. These ideas shown may be classed as revelations and sometimes coded information which may be vital to ones ministry, nation or family.

Anyone can dream, it is not limited to prophets or men of God alone e.g. Joseph,

Pharaoh, the Baker, the Butler, Abimelech and Jacob.

The Purpose of Dreams
- Dreams reveal what will happen in the future to us.

- Through dreams, God gives His children specific instructions or mandate.

- God may use dreams to give you specific instructions about some issues pertaining to your life or Nation.

- God gives us dreams when he wants to show us our purpose in life (Joseph) see: Genesis 37:10 (Pharaoh) see: Genesis 41:1.

- Dreams may forewarn somebody of an impending problem. In other words, it may serve as a protection against war, famine, giving you adequate time to prepare so that one is not caught off-guard.

We may see clear examples in the case of Pharaoh's dream which was interpreted by Joseph in Genesis 41:14-16 and also the dreams of the Butler and Baker in Genesis 40:8

Many of us have been careless about these gifts (dreams). Do you realise that many have had dreams which they forgot? Then in future, they would realise that they have seen something like that before. The beauty of this is that the moment you identify and nurture your gift with prayers, your dreams will multiply and God will continue to reveal more dreams and even strategic information, which are loaded with interpretations that could save the lives of many.

I will implore you to pray fervently to God anytime He gives you a dream - asking Him to give you the ability to interpret your dreams. Like Joseph, learn to cherish the dreams and interpretations that God gives you. The more you cherish your gifts, the more such gifts will blossom. Joseph cherished his God given gift, and that paved the way for him in life. He was not discouraged - not even when the gift put him in trouble – he still forged ahead. Note that the same gift that put him in trouble gave him success.

Joseph later became a Prime Minister in Egypt - what a great achievement, from a humble beginning.

> *"A man's gift maketh room for him and bringeth him before great men."*
> Proverbs 18:16

Develop your Gifts and Talents.
Many of our successes, achievements and failures in life lie in the God-given gifts and talents we have failed to either recognise or develop. If Biblical examples are not convincing enough, what about some great

men in our life time like our father in the Lord (Pastor Adeboye) who by God's grace is a man of God who is respected throughout the whole world. Apart from his calling as a Pastor, his gifts of the Word of Knowledge, Prophecy, and Word of Wisdom have given him a great advantage over other anointed men of God.

The fact remains that initially, nobody will believe in you during the manifestation of these gifts in your life. But don't be discouraged; sooner or later you will be recognised. All you have to do is to maintain your standard; do not lower your standard because our constant God will reward you.
Many would persecute and call you names (like Joseph's brethren called him a dreamer, mocking him). It is only the trick of the devil to distract you from your God given assignment.

> *"The thief (devil) cometh not but to steal, kill and to destroy."* John 10:10a

During the earthly ministry of our Lord Jesus Christ, he manifested the gifts of healing; he was accused by the Pharisees and Sadducees.

> *"But when Pharisees heard it, they said, This fellow doth not cast out devils, but by Beelzebub the prince of the devils."* Matthew 12:24:

Is your Dream from God?
You will soon know that your dreams are from God. This is because in due season all your interpretations will be made known to men. And the confirmation of your dreams for so many years will be established - so long as you nurture and believe in yourself and God the giver of the gifts. You will see yourself succeeding in time of chaos and difficult situations and the peace of God will keep you intact even in the face of problems. You will ride through the storms of great problems and God will be there to see you through.

As a form of illustration, I will relate the following story, from a preacher about a man who went to a chemist to find out the cost of a brain. Three brains were clearly labelled by the attendant:
• The first brains, was labelled: Anglican.
• The second brain was labelled: Catholic.
• The third brain was labelled Pentecostal.

It may surprise you to know that the most expensive one was the Pentecostal brain. You may want to ask why. A test was conducted and it was soon discovered that the Anglicans and Catholics never put their brains and faculties to task while on earth. They believe God for everything – thus, rendering their thinking faculties and God given gifts useless. That is exactly how we all behave - leaving everything to God instead of playing out God given roles.

Quite often, God's gift is there within us, sleeping, lying dormant, and waiting for the appointed time that never comes for many to tap such gifts. Yet, there are many who keep moaning that God has not blessed them. In most situations, God has implanted viable dreams in them but they are too busy to see such gifts.

Remember the story in Matthew 25:14 about talents.

> *"For unto every one that hath Shall be given, and he shall have abundance but from him that hath not shall be taken away even that which he hath!"* Matthew 25:29

I pray that such will not be your testimony; so do what you can to ensure that the gifts and potentials in you do not die a premature death. Instead, use them to glorify your creator for His wonderful works.

What would the world have lost if you were not born?

It will not surprise you to know that every good thing God created, the devil has a counterfeit. This means that you are not to believe every dream. If you over-eat, you are likely to dream of food. If you have been fasting for a long time you are likely to dream of being fed in the dream. A thirsty man dreams of water, but when a dream is repeated, you can be sure that God is telling you that he wants to do something. Moreover, there may be a specific word or lesson for you in that dream. That is why we should not ignore dreams. The Greatest Tragedies that have no remedy is to watch Gifts die untapped.

a. Imagine if Joseph died in that pit – we will not be reading about him today.

b. Imagine if his dreams never came to pass because the enemy used his brethren to frustrate his dreams, we will not use Joseph as our point of reference today.

c. Imagine that he never ended in Pharaoh's house; his destiny would have changed forever.

d. Imagine that he refused to interpret those dreams in the prison; he would have just sat there out of frustration and refused to talk to anyone. He would have even chosen to die in prison rather than use the gift that God had given to him.

We can see that Joseph had a major part to play in the scheme of God's overall plan for his life. In all that he did, he was submissive to the will of God. We will pray that God would snuff out the plans of the evil one against us and help us to achieve our dreams. We will pray fervently that God will turn the counsel of our enemies to foolishness and set us free from all his evil manoeuvrings.

PRAYER POINT

- I uproot all my buried gifts and potentials in Jesus name. I declare that the evil one will not put my God given dream into a pit like he attempted to bury Joseph's dream.

- Lord, open my eyes to see my God given talents and abilities in Jesus name. Let your dream become fresh in my heart and help me to make good use of what you have given to me.

- Oh Lord, render impotent all gifts and talent destroyers assigned to frustrate my life in the mighty name of Jesus.

- I command the moon, star and sun of my life to shine in Jesus name.

- I will not lose my calling in Jesus name; neither will I be distracted from the path that you have chosen for me.

- Oh Lord, I declare that all my stolen treasures, blessings and gifts are restored in Jesus name. Moreover I pray that they all be put in good use for the benefit of all mankind in Jesus name.

- I recall all good and useful dreams into my life in Jesus name.

- I boldly declare that all Satanic attacks aimed at me to destroy my dreams be nullified in Jesus name.

- Lord, ignite my calling with your fire in the name of Jesus.

Chapter Two

Purity: The Key to Greatness

Behold my master knoweth not what is with me in the house, and he hath committed all that he hath to my hand. There is none greater in this house than I: neither hath he kept back anything from me but thee because thou art his wife how then can I do this great wickedness, and sin against God?" Genesis 39: 8-9

Many people believe and still accept that holiness as a theme should be consigned to the past - meaning that holiness is no longer relevant to our lives today. You will agree with me that that idea is a blatant lie from the pit of hell. That is why many have compromised their faith and fallen into all types of impurity. Listen; for anyone to attain the position of greatness in life, holiness and purity are inevitable. We all know that there is the need to stay pure before marriage, and the need to deal with the flesh - that obstinate part of us that has to be dealt with. It is possible to deal with the flesh – God will give you the grace

You have to sincerely ask God to help you. Note the following points – they will do you good.

- Your ability to deny your flesh of those so-called good things will determine the level of brokenness in your life. Note that brokenness is synonymous with that discipline or submissive attitude that we require so as to achieve both physical and spiritual heights in life.

- Once you settle the issue of brokenness, you will discover that you will be able to tackle issues of spiritual warfare around you with ease.

- If you are not broken, the enemy will use those little unbroken areas in your life to torment you daily and you will not be able to excel or overcome.

- Unbroken people mess around the church, and frustrate their Pastors. The devil knows that once a Christian crosses the threshold and goes from being unbroken to being broken, the person becomes untouchable.

Therefore, one of the toughest battles you can engage in life is when you cross the threshold, then you will start to move the hand of God.

This can only be achieved when you become broken in all areas of your life.

Target for Sexual Immorality
Ephesians 6:12 clearly states:

> *"For we wrestle not against flesh and blood, but against principalities, against powers, against the rulers of the darkness of this world, against spiritual wickedness in high places."*

I will like to encourage you to be self-controlled and alert. Your enemy the devil prowls around like a roaring lion seeking for those to destroy. Look closely at the lessons that emanate from the book of 1 Peter 5:8. If you are a Pastor, Evangelist, or Deacon, note that the forces of evil have taken out a contract on you. Satan is out to get you; so if you commit immorality, the enemy would score a strategic victory in his assault on that sacred reputation that we have in Christ Jesus. Christians are a sure target of the evil one all the time. The devil has already scored victory over the unbelievers; so he is out to destroy the body of Christ purchased by his blood. The devil knows the worth and the sacrifice of Christ; that is why we should guard against all sins of the will and flesh.

Activate Discipline
Living above temptation and trials demands personal discipline. Jesus our Lord was tempted and he overcame. Joseph was nearly defiled but he fled. The Bible encourages us to flee from all forms of youthful lust. It will be very unwise to be speaking in tongues when we are confronted with a situation of sexual immorality like Joseph. He did flee; so let us emulate his example and flee. There is a time to pray, and there is a time to run. Fleeing does not make you a coward; rather, you are seen as one who is wise. (1 Corinthians 6:18).

The fault is yours
We often used the term "fall" into immorality. We do not fall into immorality. We walk into it. Immorality is a choice. It is

something that people orchestrate – they make it happen. So, we must always take responsibility for our choices and ultimate actions. If we chose to conduct our business in ministry with all diligence and discipline, God will bless our work. But if we allow immorality to taint our work, we will certainly lose the plot and not fulfil the task that the Lord has set for us. Just as Joseph did not want to disappoint God, doing all we can to remain unstained; totally committed to the task set before us.

We in the ministry play useful roles daily - caring, listening and solving problems. So in caring for others, we exude enormous charisma which attracts many to us which includes those of the opposite sex. So many ministers who are unguarded fall into the snare of lust and allow the Devil to take control. Joseph saw it coming; he knew that his dreams would be lost forever – that he would be totally destroyed – that the God that has given him those great dreams will be highly disappointed. By fleeing from that woman, he did not give the Devil the opportunity to laugh at his dreams and destroy the future plans of God.

Note that the reason why people commit sexual immorality is not just social; every sin is the trait of a tree that has a long root system. So there is always a way out; and this way out will demand your commitment - a heart determination, not lip service. If you are willing to confess and repent, that will signal the beginning of change. Repentance demands complete turnaround; complete change – a decision to do the right thing. God is counting on his ministers to stand up and be counted – to be spotless and totally sold out to the will of God – a will to commit to a life of purity and holiness.
God would have looked at Joseph and smiled; may God smile on us too.

Stay pure
Mary the mother of our Lord Jesus was highly favoured by God. Apart from Grace, she was considered pure because of her

Virginity (a Sign of Purity). Singles should learn that virginity is not old fashioned or a characteristic that does not count. God still demands this qualification in singles; you will give account of how you used your body. So, prepare to keep yourself pure as a vessel of honour in the house of God (1 Timothy 5:22). The Bible encourages us thus: "Lay hands suddenly on no man, neither be partaker of other men's sins: keep thyself pure."

According to a man of God, the purer you stay the closer you are with God. Our God dwells in Holiness Hebrews 12:14. But remember that you are prone to the attack of the devil through temptations - so be on guard. 1 Corinthians 10:12 - "Wherefore let him that thinketh he standeth take heed lest he fall. There is the tendency of thinking that you will never fall – so you are likely to expose yourself to all sorts of situations and refuse to live a well guarded life in your thoughts and actions.

My clear admonition would be simple: "LIVE HOLY, TALK HOLY AND YOU WILL DIE HOLY"

But how can you achieve a holy life? I personally think that the following points would be useful.

a. You will avoid folks that would lure you into temptation or suggest that you participate in any sin of uncleanness. Quite often, they may not come in direct ways – they will come to you indirectly. Learn to spot and avoid them like a plague.

b. You will avoid situations that will prompt you to commit sin. Do not even give such situations any consideration – neither should you give it any thought or encouragement at any time.

c. You will do all you can to let the fire of prayer to arise in your soul – meaning your will, mind and emotions must be under the control of the Holy Spirit.

d. You must train your feet to go to only the right places; don't be seen in places that will open doors to sexual immorality.

e. You must flee as previously said; you must flee physically and also train your mind and eyes to respond to things appropriately.

f. Activate the spiritual fire in you and pray without ceasing.

g. Speak it out to your spouse or Pastor as soon as any speck of evil is forming in your heart. Do not allow it to take root. Attack it as soon as possible and you will laugh with joy. Do not just pray about it – expose it by talking about it with your Senior Pastors and seek to receive counsel.

h. Refuse to stay in a lonely place where you will be attacked. Stay in the open – the devil does not like open places – he would prefer you to hide in the dark – to counsel people of the opposite sex in hidden places and for you to do things in the cover of darkness.

i. Commit your thoughts and actions to God; do not be found wanting in the speech or actions. If your words will not glorify God, do not speak it out. If your actions would not please God, do not suggest it. If your eyes will lead you to sin, pluck it out the Bible says.

j. Choose your friends carefully; it is better for you to be alone with God than to make friend with those who would lead you into all forms of immorality.

k. The Bible clearly says that friendship with the world is enmity with God. James 4:4.

PRAYER POINTS

- I command the blood of Jesus to enter into my soul and spirit and flush out every inspired thought of the devil in Jesus name.

- Lord I command every arrow of immorality released to my soul and spirit to come out by fire in the name of Jesus.

- Let my spiritual man receive the strength of God against any contact in the name of Jesus.

- Oh Lord, let the spirit that flees from sin incubate my life in Jesus name.

- Oh Lord, create in me a clean heart by your power in Jesus name.

- Father, continually give me pure Heavenly thoughts in Jesus name.

- Right now I liberate myself from any form of bondage in Jesus name.

- I break loose from any agreement with spiritual wife or husband in Jesus name.

- Lord I set my heart like a flint to destroy all their activities around me in Jesus name.

- Oh Lord, create in me a Holy anger against sin and any form of sexual immorality in Jesus name.

Chapter Three

God's Equality to Men

"Now Israel loved Joseph more than all his children, because he was 'the son of his old age: and he made him a coat of many colours'. And when his brethren saw that their father loved him more than all his brethren, they 'hated him, and could not speak peaceably unto him." Genesis 37:3-4

In the beginning, God created man in his own image by putting part of Him (God) in Adam. The initial plan of God for man was great and man was to act as little god on earth; with the ability to control, dominate, rule, create, and be productive

(Genesis 1:28). However, the devil had a plan. This is because he saw that man will gain the whole earth, and he (devil) will lose at the end. So a seed of hatred and deception was sowed in man to rebel and disobey his maker and creator (God). Since man succumbed to Satan, his dominion, authority, and privilege were withdrawn from him. But thank God that our Lord Jesus has restored and reconciled us with God through His death by shedding His blood.

> *"And that he might reconcile both unto God in one body by the cross, having slain the enmity thereby."*
> Ephesians 2:16.

It will be clearly seen that through Christ Jesus we are joint heirs to the kingdom of God. Jacob, the father of Joseph showed more affection towards him than his other brethren; an act which brought hatred towards Joseph. Looking back, could it be said that history was repeating itself again?

A flash back would reveal how Rebecca, Jacob's mother loved him more than Esau the elder brother.

> *"And Rebecca heard when Isaac spake to Esau his son. And Esau went to the field to hunt for venison, and to bring it. And Rebecca spake unto Jacob her son, saying, Behold, I heard thy father speak unto Esau thy brother, saying, Bring me venison, and make me savoury meat, that I may eat, and bless thee before the Lord before my death. Now therefore, my son, obey my voice according to that which I command thee."* Genesis 27: 5-8

As a result of the quoted verse, Jacob was nicknamed a supplanter, deceiver and a cheat; an act which nearly cost him his life and destiny.

God had to change his name from Jacob (deceiver, cheater) to ISRAEL before his purpose in life was achieved. Parents should learn from this episode not to show too much attention towards a particular child.

> *"Then Peter opened his mouth, and said, 'Of a truth I perceive that God is no respecter of persons:"* Acts 10:34

This point makes one to opine that every child is a potential star. No child should be disregarded or neglected; we need to treat them all equally because the same God created all men. (Genesis 1:25) People go around dealing with how things happened but God is simply concerned with the fact that he allowed your conception to happen.

> *"I will praise thee; for I am fearfully and wonderfully made: marvelous are thy works and that my soul knoweth right well."* Psalm 139:14.

It does not matter who your parents are or the background you come from. You are important and quite unique. The book of

Jeremiah says that before you were born, God had known you.

We really need to pray to God to discover the gifts and purpose of God in the life of our children. It is imperative to know that they have been created with different assignments in life. Some would be doctors, some teachers, lawyers, and some will be ordained to be Pastors and some Preachers and Evangelists.

Do not force any child against his or her ambition or dream. Our Lord Jesus never prayed to be a carpenter but he obeyed the will of His father (God) and His purpose was discovered in life in 1 John 3:8b: And to save the whole world from their sins. John 3:16.

Purpose
Purpose is an imperative aspect of anything. If God has plans for a nation or generation, there is always a chosen vessel – somebody that God will use to fulfil such assignments.

It is up to you to discover reasons why problems surround you. Joseph came to the realisation that God wanted to use him as a special vessel; that is why he had to pass through those tribulations. He passed through hatred, the jaws of death, blackmail, prison – all because God had a plan. Not just a plan, God had a purpose and a specific duty for his son Joseph. God wanted him to save his people from famine and starvation.

Joseph did not hate or condemn his brethren for what they did to him; neither did he curse or blame his entire predicament on his brethren who sold him to slavery. Carefully see how God showed up in his own case.

> *"And God sent me before you to preserve you a posterity in the earth, and to save your lives by a great deliverance. So now it was not you that sent me hither, but God and He had made me a father to Pharaoh, and lord of all his house and a ruler*

throughout all the land of Egypt." Genesis 45: 7-8

Moses was also raised to deliver and lead the Israelites from Egypt to the Promised Land. He went through troubles with Pharaoh - including persecution from his people. They hated him and nearly killed him.

"And Moses speak before the Lord, and saying behold the children of Israel have not hearkened unto me how then shall Pharaoh hear me, who am of uncircumcised lips?" Exodus 6:12

Jesus was born into this world to save the world from sin and to reconcile us with God whom we have lost fellowship with in Garden of Eden as the Bible says in 2 Corinthians 5:21.

"For he hath made him to be sin for us, who knew no sin; that we might be

made the righteousness of God in him."

How to Discover God's Purpose for your Life

You will discover that accusations, persecutions and enemies will rise up against your goals, plans, projects and actions. The devil will do everything in his will to frustrate that goal, Proverbs 19:21. My advice to you is that you should keep deriving pleasure in your chosen profession, calling ministry, trade, business or ventures despite the intimidation of people and the agents of the evil one. Keep enjoying the blessings that the Lord has given to you which confirms that you are on the right track. I will encourage you not to give up; be like Apostle Paul. Despite his affliction and physical attacks he still enjoyed preaching the gospel as he said:

> *"For to me to live is Christ and to die is gain."* Philippians 1:21.

Myles Munroe once said: "when man puts a limit on what he can be he has put a limit on what he will be". There is no limit to what you can achieve when you have God on your side. Remember Mark 10:27 - with God all things are possible – very possible.

If you hold on to that word, situations – like government, the weather, your job, etc, will continue to work together for your good and your purpose in God's hands will never be derailed. You will always encounter God's favour and intervention and see yourself coming out unhurt from every bad situation. God will always keep you until you fulfil your mission on earth. Romans 8:28 states:

> *"And we know that all things work together for good to them that love God, to them who are the called according to his purpose."*

"SUCCESS IS NEVER FINAL - FAILURE IS NEVER FATAL"

In all these are you willing to do the following:

a. To hold on to the word of God and insist that God's word will work for you? If you abandon the power in the word of God, you are likely going to lose the plot. The Bible says that the word of God is powerful; we need to appreciate that fact.

b. Are you willing to continue to do the will of God and never choose to do your own thing? There is the temptation for us to face more of programmes than to focus on hearing from God.

c. Have you made up your mind not to see failure as the end of the road for you? Quite often, we see failure as a point where we abandon ship - we throw in the towel – we abort all plans – we abdicate out God given roles and stop doing the will of God. We get disappointed – frustration sets in – but is that the will of God for you?

d. Have you made up your mind to pray as never before – holding onto the promises of Jesus, the rock of your salvation? You will pray till you break through; you will pray till you see your dreams turn to reality.

e. Have you decided to sing a new song in spite of all that you may be going through at this time? Ask the Holy Spirit to inspire you with new songs that will give glory to God.

f. Have you decided not to put a limit to how far you can go with God? Prepare to reach the highest heights with God.

g. Have you made up your mind to take a stand with God? God will take a stand with you too.

For the Lord GOD will help me; therefore shall I not be confounded: therefore have I set my face like a flint, and I know that I shall not be ashamed. Isaiah 50:7.

PRAYER POINTS

- Lord Almighty, fill my soul, my spirit and body with strength to operate in your kingdom in Jesus name.

- I command any stolen glory to be restored back into my life in Jesus name.

- I command the angels of the Lord to recover and restore all virtues that have been stolen from me in Jesus name.

- I reject every spirit of being the tail in Jesus name.

- I prophesy total victory over my life throughout today in Jesus name.

- I prophesy that the hand of God will be upon me all the days of my life in Jesus name.

- I terminate by fire every spirit of average today in Jesus name.

- I will rule, dominate, and control every situation around me in Jesus name.

- Every evil mark placed upon me be destroyed by fire in Jesus name.

Chapter Four

The Reality Of The Future (Imagination)

"And he told it to his father and to his brethren and his father rebuked him, and said unto him, what is this dream that thou has dreamed? Shall I and thy mother and thy brethren indeed come to bow down ourselves to thee to the earth?" Genesis 37:10

The mind is the battle ground; it occupies a very important place in a man. God's access to man is through the mind. Nothing becomes a reality in life until the mind is able to accommodate it. See 1 Peter 1: 13, which points out that we should:

a. Gird up or prepare our mind for action.
b. Take full control and responsibility of our minds.

The mind is the centre of all decisions that we take in life. Note that if you win any battle in your mind, you are likely going to win that same battle in reality. Your mind can either make you or break you. So we are supposed to watch what we allow to take root in our minds on a daily basis, so as to spoil the work of the evil one.

Let it be known today that you are the product of your thoughts. Whatever you think about would sooner or later become a reality – that is why the word of God tells us in Proverbs 4:23 to:

> *Keep thy heart with all diligence; for out of it are the issues of life.*

Proverbs 23:7: ...For as he thinketh in his heart, so is he..." In Genesis 37: 7-10, Joseph confessed the images of his dreams and future to his family; speaking them out as they occurred to him. In most cases, people would keep their dreams to themselves. But in Joseph's case, it is certain that God wanted him to speak them out. That was surely part of the plan of his future.

Imagination
The picture of the dream Joseph had dominated his mind; how do we know that? This is because we can see this clearly Genesis 37:9. Ralph Waldo Emerson opined that "A man is what he thinks all day long." That makes so much sense; as we may assume that thinking usually precedes sight. If your thought lingers for a while on anything, soon you will begin to see it clearly in your mind's eye. If you have a powerful dream in the dark, you will soon begin to see clearly.

This action of creating images in our mind is known as IMAGINATION: meaning, the ability to form images. Joseph dreamt big and he got what he conceived in his mind. The man with a great mind will one day come out with a great dream; and the man who comes out with a great dream will one day be a great man. I dare say that a man who thinks right is a man who could be seen as living in the real sense. I also believe strongly that through the dreams that God gave to Joseph, he had started devising Joseph's path to leadership - an act which started inside Joseph before it was manifested outside. Note once again – that what you see inside of you will sooner or later become a concrete reality.

Types of Mind
Our first port of call will be Romans 8:6:

> *"For to be carnally minded is death but to be spiritually minded is life and peace."*

Our mind can either be God's workshop or the devil's workshop. I am careful to encourage you to be mindful of the information you receive into your mind each day from the Television, Radio, Newspapers, Books, the Internet, Music, etc.

Think good and pure thoughts, evil thoughts pollute the mind and bring problems to our flesh. That is why Jesus said in Mark 7:18b:

> *"Do ye not perceive, that whatsoever thing from without entereth into the man, it cannot defile him."*

The word of God is our guaranteed instrument for pure thoughts. The word of God is spirit and life; it renews the mind, controls the mind, and determines the path where the mind should go.

Give attention to the word of God
Romans 12:2 encourages us not to do business with the world - in the sense of

conforming to the world. It takes the mind to conform; and conformity is an act that takes over every part of our being.

> *"And be not conformed to this world but be ye transformed by the renewing of your mind, that ye may prove what is that good, and acceptable, and perfect will of God."*

On the flip side, God wants us to be transformed – by his word. It takes the mind to be transformed. God's word builds faith within and lifts our destiny to great heights.

Philippians 2:5-11:
What type of mind does Christ possess?

> 5 *Let this mind be in you, which was also in Christ Jesus:*
> 6 *Who, being in the form of God, thought it not robbery to be equal with God: 7 But made himself of no reputation, and took upon him the form of a servant, and was made in the likeness of men:*

8 And being found in fashion as a man, he humbled himself, and became obedient unto death, even the death of the cross. 9 Wherefore God also hath highly exalted him, and given him a name which is above every name:
10 That at the name of Jesus every knee should bow, of things in heaven, and things in earth, and things under the earth; 11 And that every tongue should confess that Jesus Christ is Lord, to the glory of God the Father.

Look closely at the life of Joseph and you will see that he has similar characteristics like Jesus in the following areas:

a. He was humble through all the tribulations that he went through. He did not take any drastic step to redress issues – even when he was obviously right.

b. He suffered humiliation - in the pit – accused of rape - sent to prison; yet, he had no defence counsel but God.

c. He served with his whole heart; an act that brought glory to God and blessings to many - including those of his household.

d. After his tribulation, Joseph like our Lord Jesus had a glorious outcome at the end.

Our Lord Jesus had a unique mind that was cantered on meeting the needs of others. It may be seen thus:

a. He had a mind that thought of miracles, not obstacles; a mind that thought of possibility, not impossibility. That is why He went about doing good and saving the lost.

b. His mind thought of God's people; He accommodated love and not hate – a selfless mind that had no room for greed, and a mind that accommodated love with no trace of hatred.

c. He had a mind that was humble and not proud. He would easily have taken glory for all the wonderful things that he did on earth; but he did not. May God give us such a mind so that we would see the need to do His will and give God all the glory.

Four types of mind

It is possible to be ruled or dominated by any of these minds:
- **The Idle mind** – one that is blank and goes nowhere.
- **The Carnal mind** – aptly ruled by our
- five senses.
- **The Double mind** – not stable in anyway and thinks in opposite directions.
- **The Renewed mind** – this is the mind of Christ that thinks of solutions.

The Idle mind

It is common to see people operate within this sphere – a weakness common to many people. This type of mind runs in every direction – a mind that is known to be very unstable. It may also be said to be the devil's workshop. Why? Because it is always running to various directions like a rolling stone that has no ability to gather moss. The word IDLE means that one is not occupied or unemployed.

> *Slothfulness casteth into a deep sleep; and an idle soul shall suffer hunger.*
> Proverbs 19:15

The explanation is clear; that a mind that is not actively engaged in hardwork will invariably suffer hunger. In order words, a mind that is disconnected or not engaged with thinking upon accurate things will suffer hunger. So, when you allow your mind to wonder instead of being engaged with truth, you think about things over and over without being fully engaged in anything. That is a clear indication that we should spend time to fill our hearts with the word of God; which is able to take the hunger for the things of the world away from us.

The Carnal mind
If you operate with this sort of mind, your emotions and senses will definitely misguide

you. You can't trust them because they will lead you astray; you can only trust the word of God. Thinking on things that your senses tell you are contrary to the word of God. It leads to death.

> *5 For they that are after the flesh do mind the things of the flesh; but they that are after the Spirit the things of the Spirit. 6 For to be carnally minded is death; but to be spiritually minded is life and peace. 7 Because the carnal mind is enmity against God: for it is not subject to the law of God, neither indeed can be.*
> *8 So then they that are in the flesh cannot please God. 9 But ye are not in the flesh, but in the Spirit, if so be that the Spirit of God dwell in you. Now if any man have not the Spirit of Christ, he is none of his.* Romans 8:5-9

The Double mind
The double minded person is someone who is "unstable in all his ways" James 1:8. He

cannot make up his mind. One minute he is spiritual minded (thinking on the word of God) and the next minute he is carnal minded – allowing his senses to take control. Thus, people who are controlled by their senses will not go far with God. Why? Because they are always looking at their feelings. Note that when we are controlled by elements of our feelings, we tend to allow the flesh to rule over our nature.

Such a double minded person would be led by what the world says about any given situation; soon they would change their position and be led by what the natural things of the world dictate to them. This constant change from one direction to another makes such a person to be constantly fickle minded or inconsistent. You will always find that they are indecisive, as they constantly change their position.

A transformation may be necessary; but such a transformation of mind from being a double minded person to being single minded in Spirit may not happen overnight. However, if you persevere and make up your mind to move from one level to the other, you will become a vessel unto honour.

The Renewed mind
The spirit man is born again the moment you receive salvation, but the mind is renewed through a gradual process, of transformation. Your mind was originally contaminated and corrupted with sin, when your spirit was born again, God's word started transforming and renewing your mind. Therefore the accuracy of your thinking is increased proportionately to the degree of your alignment with God's word. If a thought penetrates your mind and it doesn't align with the word, it doesn't belong there. You should reject it. I will encourage you to consistently think about things that are lovely, delightful and in harmony with God's word; nothing contrary. Think deeply about the fact that virtue is a life giving substance. If something

ministers life to you, that is what you should be thinking about or concentrating your thoughts upon.

The word of God reflects upon what goes on within your heart.

Positive Confession
> Proverbs 18:21: *"Death and life are in the power of the tongue..."*

You are what you say you are. Your confession matters a lot in life. God had to speak out His word into our system before it became a reality. So be positive in your speech. As a Child of God your tongue carries power to do whatever you send it to do. See: Isaiah 55:11.

> *So shall my word be that goeth forth out of my mouth: it shall not return unto me void, but it shall accomplish that which I please, and it shall prosper in the thing whereto I sent it.*

Remember that Joseph had dreams; he confessed his dreams continuously to his brethren. Because he confessed his dream, it became a reality – we can really testify to that. Do not bother about the paths that took him to the realisation of his dreams; this is because many Christians expect that the path to their success will be paved with gold. That is not the way God works.

Moses did not have a party as he marched the Israelites out of Egypt into the Promised Land. Our Lord and saviour Jesus Christ went to the Cross to secure our salvation; that was not a picnic; it took toil, sweat, stripes, blood and being nailed to the cross. Joseph did not have a smooth ride either – he started from a pit and landed in a lovely setting and soon found himself in prison before he tasted royalty.

It is clear that the mind speaks from the resources that are embedded in the mind.
- Speak good things to yourself and situations around you all the time.

- Do not be caught speaking negative words about your situation and circumstances.
- Let your words inspire the deep roots of faith in you.

David had already prophesied killing Goliath before the battle was won according to his words. 1 Samuel 17:46. According to Pastor E.A. Adeboye, *"You are a product of what you said about yourself years ago. What you will be in future is what you are saying about yourself now" As for me I know I am going to be great in life. I say these to myself every day. What about you?*

Time and Season
We really have to take into consideration the time of performance of those things you have prophesied concerning your life. Patience plays a key role. There is a time to plant and a time to sow Ecclesiastes 3: 1-2.

Study the life of great men of valour in the book of destiny (Bible) and you will find that one common thing about them was their ability to wait upon the promises of God.

Between the period of your spoken word and your eventual performance is the period of patience. When you believe God and His promise you need not be in haste. Abraham was not in haste; he was sure that what God promised him will be fulfilled. The story of the fig tree is an example. Jesus spoke to the tree, and by the time they came back, it had dried up.

Joseph's time of performance was 22 years between his confession and the realisation of his dream. What you can be sure about is that God never fails in his promises; it might be delayed but will never be denied. What happens in many cases, many people give up and refuse to wait patiently. Joseph would have abandoned his dreams – he waited.

PRAYER POINTS

- Lord, give me the eyes of an Eagle so I can see better than what I can see now.

- Let my spiritual eyes and ears be wide opened in the name of Jesus.

- Lord anoint my eyes so that they may see and hear wondrous things from heaven.

- Holy Spirit, control my ability to frame my words right in the name of Jesus.

- I declare that every battle standing ahead my future be destroyed in Jesus name.

- I render and destroy every weapon used to monitor my future and render such weapons powerless in Jesus name.

- I cancel all the negative confessions that may stand against my destiny now and in future in Jesus name.

- I declare that my miracle will not pass me by in Jesus name.

- Lord I break every stronghold of delay to my breakthrough in Jesus name.

Chapter Five

Opposition Against our Vision

"And Joseph dreamed a dream, and he told it his brethren: and they hated him yet the more." Genesis 37:5

Every good and great vision will be opposed either by the devil or people around you. But we must rejoice when opposition comes our way. By so doing, it brings the best out of us. Opposition makes you to aspire, pray more, be creative and keep you moving towards the ladder of success. Don't run away from opposition but resist by discovering a way of escape.

Our gifts are discovered when our destiny is challenged; and potentials are released. Oranges are sweet, but you have to squeeze and suck before the best (Juice) comes out of it. When we want the best out of life, give room for challenges – they will help you to grow. Joseph was not only opposed by his family; he was harassed by Potiphar's wife, who put Joseph in trouble. Joseph never complained or murmured.

Moreover, Joseph never accused his brethren of being the cause of his problem. He accepted opposition. Jesus Christ our Lord was opposed by Peter (Asst. Pastor on his earthly ministry) the same Peter who confessed Jesus as Son of God was rebuked by Jesus for being used of Satan. Why? Peter wanted to stand against the will of God in the life of Jesus. Matthew 16:17, 23.

Be Victorious

If there is no competition, there will be no winner. You can only be declared a winner when you have won a battle against an opponent. Great folks do not run away from obstacles or opposition; they use such as stepping stones or ladder of Success. Have you ever heard that quitters don't win and winners don't quit?

Only those who endure till the end shall be saved. Note also that Salvation is free, but somebody paid the price before you could enjoy it. And remember that you have a role to play if you want to make Heaven. Victory is of the Lord (By strength shall no man prevail).

The only guarantee for safety and victory is the presence of God around you. The Bible records that the favour (presence) of God was with Joseph. Genesis 39:2: *"And the Lord was with Joseph, and he was a prosperous man and he was in the house of his master the Egyptian."*

Know your God
The amount of victory you get is determined by the Godly forces backing you, and the strength and power that support you during your time of opposition. Daniel 11:32b: explains that *"...the people that do know their God shall be strong, and do exploits."*

Remember how in 1 Kings 18, the false prophets of Baal challenged the God of Elijah to battle; that was at their own risk and peril. They all died and that is a good lesson for all the forces of the evil one that are enraged against us in one way or the other.

We all know that our God has never lost a battle and will never lose one. I pity those who are far away from God. Their lives are in great danger. I will encourage you to join forces with the winners; team up with the Lord's army and be assured of victory. In all you do, do not forget this important Bible verse:

> Psalm 127:1: *"Except the Lord build the house, they labour in vain that build it."*

PRAYER POINTS

- I declare that every wall of demarcation between me and success be pulled down in Jesus name.

- Oh Lord! I command every Goliath standing on my way to be slain and I command the mouth of the lions in my life to be shut in Jesus name.

- I command every evil wind blowing in my life, family, and business to cease now in Jesus name.

- I declare that all curses working against my destiny be broken in Jesus name and I take authority against every strongman of progress in my life in the name of Jesus.

- Arise oh Lord and scatter all my enemies in Jesus name - Lord let the way of my enemies be dark and slippery now – amen.

- I break all power of occultism working to frustrate my Christian life, and I command victory in all parts of my life in Jesus name.

Chapter Six

There shall be a Performance

"And Joseph was the governor over the land, and he it was that sold to all the people of the land and Joseph's brethren came, and bowed down themselves before him with faces to the earth." Genesis 42:6

At God's appointed time he brings fulfilment and performance to what we believe, confess or imagined. Habakkuk 2:3:

> *"For the vision is yet for an appointed time, but at the end it shall speak, and not lie: though it tarry, wait for it;*

because it will surely come, it will not tarry."

If it took many years for Joseph to realise his dreams, I can assure you that you will reach your goal. God does not count days or years in his agenda; a thousand years may seem like a day. A sister once said that she had been married for 6 years with no child. Another brother said he believes he should get married between the age of 28 and 30. How is he sure that he knows God's approved timing?

The Bible says (God seated in Heaven doing whatever pleases him at his time). One thing I have appreciated God for in my life is that God is never late in a situation and always constant. God's time is the appointed time. The weather, time, situation and people around you may change but God remains the same and no man or prayer can be offered to change God's mind. Hebrews 13:8.

Prayers don't change God but prayers can change our problems to miracles and our obstacles to testimonies. We ought to pay more attention to prayers; prayers will open any door; who is behind all miracles? God.

> Malachi 3:6: *"For I am the Lord, I change not therefore ye sons of Jacob are not consumed."*

Time of Performance

Pay attention to the words of the Psalmist. This was not a cry of despair but of joy and victory.

> *"When the Lord turned again the captivity of Zion We were like them that dream. Then was our mouth filled with laughter, and our tongue with singing then said they among heathen, the Lord has done great things for them."* Psalm 126:1-2:

The time of performance can reveal the following in the life of a Christian:

- It is a time of jubilation
- A time of relaxation
- A time of fulfilment when you now look back and count your blessings.
- A time to offer thanksgiving to God who delivered you from snare of the fowler.
- A time of deliverance when your heart is full of praise for Jehovah the Lord of Host.

Beloved, it doesn't matter whoever is obstructing your goal; you will prevail at God's appointed time. If it takes nine months for pregnant woman to deliver a child, God will also see you through your heavy burden. You will agree that they carry a great and heavy burden. But when delivery time comes, people rejoice and celebrate with them.

There might be nobody to console you at the time of your problem; like Joseph had nobody to help him except God. There was no brother, sister, father or mother to help;

he solely depended on God – the author and finisher of his dreams. There was no one to support or give him words of encouragement, except God.

Remember what Prophet Isaiah said:

> *"But now thus saith the LORD that created thee, O Jacob, and he that formed thee, O Israel, Fear not: for I have redeemed thee, I have called thee by thy name; thou art mine. When thou passest through the waters, I will be with thee; and through the rivers, they shall not overflow thee: when thou walkest through the fire, thou shalt not be burned; neither shall the flame kindle upon thee. For I am the LORD thy God, the Holy One of Israel, thy Saviour: I gave Egypt for thy ransom, Ethiopia and Seba for thee. ...But be assured of victory.* Isaiah 43: 1-3.

In Genesis 37:6-7, Joseph dreamt and in Genesis 44:14 & Genesis 50:18 the time of performance and fulfilment came. Your own time of performance concerning God's promises in your life will manifest in Jesus name. Notice that Joseph alone shared in his problems but when victory and fulfilment came, his brothers located him.

Your enemy will bow to you in Jesus Name. Joseph had the solution to problems of his family. You will feed your enemies and they will be put to shame.

> *Proverbs 16:7: When a man's ways please the LORD, he maketh even his enemies to be at peace with him.*

Faith in God's Word
> *"And blessed is she that believed: for there shall be a performance of those things which were told her from the Lord."* Luke 1:45

Our faith is the determinant factor towards our destiny. Be it unto you according to your faith. Your faith will help you to reject bad dreams or evil reports. Faith determines your decision; your decision determines your destiny. Your faith helps you to channel your prayers to the right course.

> *"Trust in the LORD with all thine heart; and lean not unto thine own understanding. In all thy ways acknowledge him, and he shall direct thy paths."* Proverbs 3:5-6

Let us trust God for who He is; not what we feel or people say about us and our conditions. Mary, the mother of Jesus was a virgin; yet she believed God for a child; what a wonderful woman. But some married woman will still doubt God for their situation. Sisters, I challenge you to change your confession today that you are blessed and fruitful.

Today, I will like to encourage you to accept God by his words, and it shall be well with you.

THERE SHALL SURELY BE A PERFORMANCE IN YOUR LIFE IN JESUS NAME AMEN.

PRAYER POINTS

- I declare every arrow of discouragement sent against my soul broken in Jesus name.

- Holy Ghost, make me a candidate of miracles in Jesus name.

- I command ever spirit that is responsible for the abortion of miracles in my life to be paralysed in Jesus name.

- Oh Lord, confront every battle that is older than my age and destroy every evil power working against my destiny in Jesus name.

- Holy Ghost locate me to my place of breakthrough and destroy every sickness and disease the enemy has introduced to my body in Jesus name.

- Lord I put stumbling blocks in the realm of the spirit against all my enemies in Jesus name.

- Lord, I decree disappearance among all the enemies who decide to hold secret meetings concerning me in Jesus name.

- I hereby decree that there will be a performance in my life in Jesus name. I believe that God will make all my dreams come to pass and the Glory will return to him – amen.

- I come against every spirit of the evil one that would prevent my dreams from becoming a reality in Jesus name.

- I confirm by faith that a time of fulfilment will come to pass in my life and many will come to celebrate my success in Jesus name.

- Lord I hereby release my thanksgiving to you in advance, knowing that I will prevail in Jesus name. Thanks for delivering me from the hands of evil snares and the hands of the fowler in Jesus name.

Chapter Seven

Forgiveness

"So shall ye say unto Joseph, Forgive, I pray thee now, the trespass of thy brethren, and their sin; for they did unto thee evil: and now, we pray thee, forgive the trespass of the servants of the God of thy father. And Joseph wept when they spake unto him...."
Genesis 50: 17

Joseph's brethren fell down before him, asking for forgiveness. Joseph was very magnanimous - holding out his hand of love to them. This great lesson shows that forgiving those who have wronged you is a key to personal peace. The only way to free our mind from trouble is to avoid any resentment and abhor no evil thought within us. It is far better to forgive and forget than to hate and remember.

Unforgiveness blocks us from receiving our blessings. Note that forgiveness will not change the past, but it will enlarge the future; so do not burn bridges – you will be surprised how many times you will have to cross over that same bridge over and over again. Ask God to teach you how to maintain your bridges by the special grace of God.

If God would only open our eyes to the future; we would be wiser than we are today. We will not judge and we will do all we can to live in peace with all.

> Luke 6:37: *"Judge not, and ye shall not be judged: condemn not, and ye shall not be condemned: forgive, and ye shall be forgiven."*

Some of us may have had bitter experiences from our friends, brethren, and parents in the past – just like what Joseph went through. We have been hurt so much that the mind is polluted with evil thoughts towards the person or people involved.

But as a child of God, it is wrong to feel that way. Think of God our father and imagine how many times we fail him in our responsibilities and our act of disobedience to his will.; yet God is merciful toward us. Psalm 130:3: *"If thou, LORD, shouldest mark iniquities, O Lord, who shall stand?"*

Let God have his way
Nothing happens without Gods approval in our life. Tough situations and temptations may come our way in order for God to teach

us some lesson and correct our ways of living. We should ask ourselves these questions anytime someone hurts our feelings:

- Have I ever hurt someone before?
- Suppose I am the one in the other person's shoes? Or suppose it was the other way
- Do I have a lesson to learn from this bitter round?
  experience?

As long as we depend on the flesh for our results, there will be more failure. But when the Spirit of God takes control and dominates our lives, there will be good news and good results. Moreover, a better character is released from our person. Galatians 5:16, 22.

I can safely counsel that if you rely on the Holy Spirit, you will find it easy to overlook the people that step on your toes. A brother confessed after listening to someone –

saying that he had been keeping the records of the wife's offences in a Diary. However, if you will remind yourself that it's by the mercy of God that you are not consumed. The Bible commands that we submit ourselves one to another in the fear of God - Ephesians 5:21. Did the Bible in Ephesians 5:25 not say that husbands should love their wives even as Christ also loved the church, and gave himself for it; such should be our perfect example.

The Mercy of God
There is no sin that is too much for God to pardon. Christ was sent to die on the Cross of Calvary to shed His blood so that we will obtain mercy. Sin came through a man, (Adam) mercy and forgiveness came through another man. (Jesus). Psalm 130:8: "He (Jesus) shall redeem Israel from all his iniquities."

Remember the woman who committed adultery in John 8: 1-11. This story is a good lesson to everyone that there is no one that is guiltless and as the Bible says "all have sinned and come short of glory of God" but Jesus being the Master that is above law did not condemn the woman but pardoned her sins.

> *John 8:11: "And Jesus said unto her, "Neither do I condemn thee: go, and sin no more."*

If God could pardon our sin and iniquity who is man to condemn and not to forgive? Man finds it easy to accuse, condemn and prosecute, not mindful of their own attitude and reactions towards the other party. Remember the parable of the unforgiving servant? Look closely if you can identify yourself in the picture painted in the Bible. *23 Therefore is the kingdom of heaven likened unto a certain king, which would take account of his servants.*

> *24 And when he had begun to reckon, one was brought unto him, which owed him ten thousand talents.*

25   But forasmuch as he had not to pay, his lord commanded him to be sold, and his wife, and children, and all that he had, and payment to be made.

26   The servant therefore fell down, and worshipped him, saying, Lord, have patience with me, and I will pay thee all.   27 Then the lord of that servant was moved with compassion, and loosed him, and forgave him the debt.

28   But the same servant went out, and found one of his fellowservants, which owed him an hundred pence: and he laid hands on him, and took him by the throat, saying, Pay me that thou owest.

29   And his fellowservant fell down at his feet, and besought him, saying, Have patience with me, and I will pay thee all.   30 And he would not: but went and cast him into prison, till he should pay the debt. 31 So when his fellowservants saw what was done, they were very sorry, and came and told unto their lord all that was done.

32 Then his lord, after that he had called him, said unto him, O thou wicked servant, I forgave thee all that debt, because thou desiredst me:

33 Shouldest not thou also have had compassion on thy fellowservant, even as I had pity on thee?

34 And his lord was wroth, and delivered him to the tormentors, till he should pay all that was due unto him.

35 So likewise shall my heavenly Father do also unto you, if ye from your hearts forgive not every one his brother their trespasses. Matthew 18: 23-35

Joseph's brethren discovered their error and apologised. In Genesis 50: 17-18 they all felt sorry, apologised and gave honour to Joseph according to the dream Joseph had. But Joseph, a man filled with God's Spirit, did not speak hastily nor did he use the opportunity to maltreat or take revenge; an attitude common to men, encouraging us to act on: Hebrew 12:14a. "Follow peace with all men."

Joseph understood by experience that when God fights for someone, he gives total victory. God is the Lord of host who cannot lose a battle. That is why I am sure as many that are being persecuted, humiliated by your household, that God will give you victory. Amen.

So Joseph's case teaches us a lesson. He did not only forgive his brethren but also saved them from death (famine), fed them and brought relief to his descendants.

A clear case in point is the destructive power of anger; a tool that the devil uses to destroy many children of God. Anger destroys many things, anger does not see solutions.

The power of forgiveness
Anger is controlled by the devil and anger brings more hatred. Anger will not bring

progress. Each time anger comes your way, deal with the spirit as fast as you can and get rid of it.

- Forgiveness releases you; creates freedom and brings the peace of God into your heart.
- Forgiving those who have wronged you is a key to personal peace.
- The secret of a long and fruitful life is to forgive everybody.
- It is far better to forgive and forget than to hate and remember.
- To remember old offences is like putting our heads in a noose or putting ourselves in chains.
- If Joseph had decided not to forgive his brethren, he would have lost all that God wanted to achieve through him and his dream would not have been a reality.
- Unforgiveness blocks blessings; forgiveness releases blessings.
- Forgiveness won't change the past, but it will enlarge the future.
- Forgiveness breaks chains off people; it frees many from the bondage of the mind. It is one act that frees the person

offering it, and the person that it is being offered to.
- Forgiveness gives one a new lease of life. It gives people the opportunity to start gain and see things from a new perspective. Is that not what salvation does to us? It gives us the opportunity to start on a clean slate – to begin again and turn from our wicked ways to righteousness.
- Forgiveness, if well managed, creates a new being; as we see the birth of a new being. Such a person begins to appreciate life in a new way and begins to set things straight – better than they had done before. So if we have a choice, we would rather forgive as many people as possible so that the world would become a better place for all.

Our Lord Jesus was crucified for the sin he never committed, but because of the glory ahead, He endured, the suffering. Luke 23:34: "Then Jesus said, 'Father, forgive them, for they know not what they do'. And they parted his raiment, and cast lots."

PRAYER POINTS

- Father, I cancel every sin that stands against my progress with the blood of Jesus - amen.

- I decree the mercy of Jehovah over my life in Jesus name.

- Let the beauty and glory of Jehovah cover me in Jesus name.

- I refuse to eat the bread of sorrow all my life in Jesus name.

- Oh Lord let the spirit of forgiveness flow into my adversary in Jesus name.

- You spirit of Hatred and Anger against my destiny die in Jesus name.

- Lord, create in me spirit that hates sin and unrighteousness in Jesus name.

- Lord I pray that your love and peace will arise in my heart against those that seek to plot my downfall in Jesus name.

- Love I receive the grace to love those that hate me in Jesus name.

Chapter Eight

Love Your Enemies

"And Joseph said unto them, fear not for am I in the place of God. But as for you ye thought evil against me, but God meant it unto good, to bring it to pass as it is this day to save much people alive. Now therefore, fear ye not, I will nourish you and your little ones. And he comforted them and spake kindly unto them." Genesis 50: 19-21

The Bible has in various instances encouraged the Children of God to love their enemies. This is a very bitter pill to swallow. They often wonder why they should love those who have caused them a great deal of pain. However, when God opens our spiritual eyes, to show us who our real enemies are, we will know that the focus of our prayer needs to be changed.

Looking at the story of Joseph, we may conclude that the brethren of Joseph were his enemy. But if you look deeply, why will a blood brother derive pleasure in killing his brother? Something should tell us there is a force behind that evil action - the devil. See John 10:10.

The devil is behind every evil action taken by anybody on the face of the earth.

Note the following perspectives of how far the devil would go:
   a. Who causes forceful suggestions that give rise to the spirit of anger?

b. Who causes the hatred that rises among brethren?
c. What makes folks not to appreciate all the kindness you show to them?
d. Why do many seek to derive sexual pleasure outside their God ordained marriage, or seek to enjoy the fruit of fornication instead of getting married?
e. Why do many people seek to cheat others while using the name of God?
f. Why is there so much hatred to the extent that some would kill those they hate to the core?

It is the devil who comes to kill, steal and destroy. As soon as you realise that he has a plan to destroy the work of God, you are half way through defeating him. Joseph saw the hand of the evil one – he had a dream – he knew that God had a plan for his life – he did not want to defile himself and offend that great God that brought him out of that pit – so he stayed on God's side. Would you choose to shame Satan and give glory to God?

I will encourage Pastors and deliverance ministers to look beyond casting out fire and brimstone from many Christians. The target that needs dealing with is the Devil – the one we have identified as the spoiler – not people. It is the devil at work, trying to soil the good work of God.

> *"For we wrestle not against flesh and blood, but against principalities, against powers, against the rulers of the darkness of this world, against spiritual wickedness in high places."*
> Ephesians 6:12

Discover the source of the problem

In all my days as a Christian, I can categorically affirm that there is no problem that God cannot solve. The word of God is clear on this matter. God can solve all problems. Listen; as soon as you find yourself in any problem, let your first port of call be prayer.

Open that channel of communication with God and locate the source of the problem with God's help. Joseph was able to identify his source of problem and so he knew the problem will not kill or terminate his life. In Genesis 50:20 he knew that his enemy was the cause of his predicament, so he renewed his hope in God.

Take a close look at the word of God and see how we are supposed to react to problems and temptations.

> 1 Corinthians 10:13: *"There hath no temptation taken you but such as is common to man: but God is faithful, who will not suffer you to be tempted above that ye are able: but will with the temptation also "make a way to escape, that ye may be able to bear it."*

Do not be surprised – learn a lesson here and learn it as fast as you can; the righteous will be persecuted, jailed, assaulted, accused of the sin or offence never committed - but God is always with the righteous in all situations. The righteous might fall many times but will surely rise up and not stay down. The idea is that the devil will like you to stay down, to be totally frustrated – to imagine that God has lost his power to act on your behalf and unlike Joseph, one would have abandoned the dream and seen God as a liar and one who does not answer prayers.

>Psalm 34:19: *"Many are the afflictions of the righteous; but the LORD delivereth him out of them all."*

Our back-up
Most computers have a very important element or a programme known as the back-up. Who is your back up?. Your victory in life depends on an effective and reliable back-up and the strength and capacity they have to support you. If God the all sufficient is your back-up, you need not entertain fear.

He has never lost a battle before; neither will he lose the battle concerning you. Your victory is certain if you totally link up with Him. See Psalm 18:48. Only Jesus can guarantee safety from all enemies.

Locating Christ in the midst of crisis
There is always a saying that a life without Christ is in crisis. The only man free from crisis is the man having the spirit of God in him (Jesus Christ). In every problem, let us locate God clearly; let us not dwell on the problem. You will soon realise that problems are made to challenge us – build us – make us stronger - move us forward – to train us more – to open doors for our promotion like in the case of Joseph.

> *"But put ye on the Lord Jesus Christ, and make not provision for the flesh, to fulfil the lusts thereof."* Romans 13:14:

Let go – let God...

If we really have to walk in the love of God, we have to learn to dwell in forgiveness. Although this may be difficult, we must learn to take hold with God and do what he would do – love.

Note that it is easier to hate than to forgive; and we may see an example from the life of Christ. When Jesus was teaching the disciples about retaliation and love in Matthew 5:44, he commanded them (including us) to love their enemies and to always pray for them. So the lesson is clear; if there is someone in your family who is not a Christian, you still have to love them. The starting point would be to intercede on their behalf and continually pray for them. Know that their salvation lies within your reach.

Jesus Christ never for once cursed or picked up a fight when betrayed by Judas Iscariot. If God be for us, who can be against us? Nobody can be against you and every opposition against you will be totally shattered in Jesus name. Cursing, binding people and calling fire on them from heaven when we think they are our enemies is not right. Moreover, the binding and planning for the destruction of those we see as our enemies was not commanded by Jesus.

Love does not hurt, love does not grumble, love does not retaliate, love does not fight back, love does not curse or wish others evil, or wish that bad things would happen to those who hate us or treat us despitefully.

On the flip side, love seeks for the good of those who plot evil against us – love is kind to those who hate us – love shares – love gives and like Joseph shows, love is patient and is kind even in the pit, in prison and in the palace.

Furthermore, love will always find a way to assist his brethren. Love lasts longer than hatred. Read Genesis 50: 19-21. I pray that God will give us (believers) the type of spirit in Joseph; a Christ - like spirit.

Chapter Nine

Exploring the Five Pillars
Linked With Joseph

Paternal

Joseph's problem may be partly associated to one of his parents. Many Bible scholars will blame the part that his father played as responsible for the problem of hatred that arose among Joseph's siblings. So many would point out that even the idea of the coat of many colours is associated with selective love. They would argue that if his father did not show that he loved Joseph particularly, the idea of hatred would not have risen among his siblings. But in all these, we will not fail to see the hand of God at work.

We cannot deny the fact that Joseph had dreams – but his brothers were bent on showing their old parent that Joseph would not be their Lord and master – so they would never bow to him. Did the old man know their plans? No. It makes sense to discover the source of your problems before praying, so as to know the right approach.

If Joseph's father, Jacob had prayed, could things have happened differently? Who knows?

Paternal problem could come inform of direct attack to one's life and career. You might see yourself succeeding or manifesting a gift above your brethren, watch it. Hatred may set in, be vigilant and wise in approaching issues that relate to your relations. They are closer to you and know your secrets and your weakness. Esau was by natural law to be the Elder but through hatred and preference of Jacob to Esau, Rebecca planned to sell Esau's birthright to Jacob. Genesis 27: 5-9. The Bible warns us in Matthew 10:36. Paternal Problems could arise in so many ways, David and Absalom; a son wanting to kill his father what an evil world.

Pit

There are certain problems we cannot avoid in life. Some of these problems may be natural – occurring without human interference. In some cases, prayer and fasting will not help. Such problems are destined to come so that the scripture may be fulfilled in one's life. Moreover some problems are inevitable – but when we pray, God is able to intervene.

However, servants of God will always say, prayers do not change God, but prayer changes our situations. When Jesus prayed in Garden of Gethsemane, one would have thought God will reverse His decision; instead it was like Jesus was abandoned. Did it not seem that Joseph would be abandoned in the pit? God intervened because there was a purpose for him in the future.

Potiphar

The Potiphar problem can be likened to temptation in the life of the children of God. Potiphar's wife tempted Joseph but, Joseph refused to yield because he did not want to sin against God – choosing to stay pure and holy. Note that temptation is bound to come the way of believers; but your reaction to the situation would determine your stand with God. But God commands us to flee from sin

> 1 Corinthians 6:18: *"Flee fornication, Every sin that a man doeth is without the body; but he that committeth fornication sinneth against his own body."*

Remember that Judas Iscariot was tempted with money and he yielded to the temptation.

He accepted to be used by the devil and clearly destroyed his destiny. David, a man of valour saw the nakedness of Bathsheba from afar and instead of fleeing, fell and committed adultery. Note that temptation will come in many ways through women, money, lust etc. Ministers of God need to be careful because they are prone to all sorts of attacks. Once again, the devil comes to kill, steal and destroy. Do you think the devil will fold his arms and see millions marching to heaven?

Prison

Joseph was put into a pit – a sort of temporary prison, not because he committed any offence. He was sent to prison and suffered the humiliation of being called an ungrateful and evil person – but he did not deserve a place in prison. But in all these, we can trace the roots of his problems. His brethren hated him to the point of death;

every step and action he took resulted into hatred. But did God fight for him? Yes. Relate this to yourself. Persecution will come because of your talent or position. If you are the lonely voice in the desert like John the Baptist, you are going to be hated if you preach hot sermons and ask sinners to repent. That is why his head was cut off and put on a platter for preaching against Herod.

So your imprisonment may come as a result of preaching the gospel, and walking in righteousness of God like Paul and Silas who were thrown into prison. Remember that Peter was persecuted and imprisoned for preaching about Jesus. But the beauty of it is that persecution is meant to toughen and strengthen us, and bring us closer to knowledge of God. Joseph was imprisoned for a sin he never committed - an attempt by the devil to cut short his destiny, but God made Joseph a leader in that prison yard.

Palace

Palaces are made for Kings - not slaves. In the palace, you are bound to live in abundance, majesty, grandeur and authority. Men and nations will serve you and honour you. I desire to be in a Palace all the days of my life. The palace is a place of glory where shame and reproach is removed; tears and weeping are terminated. It was not a mistake that Joseph found himself in a palace; it was ordained by God. No matter what your enemies do or plan against you, you will reach your Goal. I am heading for the mountain top – I am heading for the top of the mountain and not the valley. The Bible says "I will be the head not the tail, above not beneath." Deuteronomy 28:13.

If you are living below your potential pray that God will locate you to the Palace where your enemy will bow down before you; where you will control the wealth, riches, and economy of nations, I desire to be there. Beloved, Joseph was made second in command to Pharaoh; a Prime Minister. God is no respecter of persons, we are told in the scriptures – and if God can make this happen for Joseph because he held on to God, he will also do it for you. THERE SHALL SURELY BE A PERFORMANCE concerning those dreams, goals and visions that God has planted in you.

I will encourage you to prepare to launch out with God; but I will like you to know that no victory comes without pain – roses have thorns – yet they are sweet smelling and beautiful. Joseph did not walk through a smooth path – so do not expect that it will be smooth sailing for you even now. Brethren, when you have been tried and tested like raw gold, God will make you shine. Your day of performance is at hand and the gates of Hell will not prevail against your victory. Open your eyes my brethren and see where God is taking you; prepare to stay in the will of God. I'll see you at the top.

PRAYER POINTS

- I hereby come against every incantation or negative words that may be uttered against me; I declare them impotent, in the name of Jesus

- I pursue and overtake all my enemies and I recover every property that have been stolen from me in the name of Jesus.

- I come against all the raging storms in my life, and I ask them to be still in the name of Jesus.

- Today, I pray against whatever will not make the desire and expectation of God to come upon my life in Jesus name

- I hereby come against all forces of the enemy that would plan to push me into any pit or prison. I pray that all their plans against me are destroyed in Jesus name.

- I pray against every enemy of Joy in my life in the name of Jesus. I declare that God will bring me to my palace, where there shall be a great performance in Jesus name.